THE
LAST FEW

James Eckersley

PUBLISHED BY

DouglasHouse

First published in the UK by Douglas House in 2005

© Douglas House
PO Box 396
Tonbridge. TN9 9BB. UK

Aircrew portrait photographs ©James Eckersley 2005
Book and cover design by James Eckersley

RAF Squadron Insignia reproduced with the kind
permission of Her Majesty's Stationary Office.
©Crown Copyright / Ministry of Defence

Portrait Drawing of P/O. J. Bisdee by Cuthbert Orde.
Reproduced with the kind permission of Cuthbert Orde's Family.
©Cuthbert Orde's Estate.
With thanks to The Royal Air Force Museum.

HRH Prince Michael of Kent portrait ©HRH Prince Michael of Kent.

Pre-interview research from the following publications:
"Men of the Battle of Britain" By Kenneth G. Wynn
First published in 1989 by Giddon Books. ISBN 0 947893156.
"....So Few". Written by John Golley.
Copyright - W H Smith 1992. ISBN 0 906782 92 9.

A catalogue record for this book is available
from the British Library

ISBN 0-9550080-0-X

To the memory of the men who took part in this project, but sadly died before its completion.

Foreword by

HRH Prince Michael of Kent GCVO.

KENSINGTON PALACE,
LONDON,W.8.

It is unusual nowadays to find any remaining gap in the coverage of the activities of Fighter Command during the Battle of Britain. 'The Last Few' is a remarkable collection of photographs of those surviving members of The Few - pilots, navigators, ground crew - whose contribution to the outcome of the war are here described.

It is a personal dossier of the heroic exploits of these extraordinary people and a moving testament to their gallantry.

Michael

The Battle of Britain

In the summer of 1940 the most decisive aerial conflict in British history was fought in the skies over Southern England. The men who fought were often teenagers fresh out of flight training, but they proved to be legendary aviators whose exploits are now revered throughout the world.

With the fall of France and the evacuation of the British Expeditionary Forces from the beaches of Dunkirk, Nazi Germany planned the final stages of its domination of Western Europe - Britain stood alone as Adolf Hitler prepared 'Operation Sealion', the planned military assault on the United Kingdom from the sea and air.

"..... the Battle for France is now over. I expect the Battle of
Britain is about to begin. Upon this battle depends the
survival of Christian civilisation".

(Winston Churchill. June 1940)

The coastal defenses of Southern England were hastily strengthened, but Hitler knew that air supremacy over the English Channel was the essential element for a successful invasion, for without it the Royal Air Force could attack any invasion fleet before it ever reached British soil.

Hermann Göring, Head of the German Luftwaffe, was charged with the quick and decisive destruction of the RAF both in the air and on the ground. He anticipated this would take no longer than four weeks to achieve and in the summer of 1940 he sent over wave after wave of German fighters and bombers to pound RAF aircraft, airfields and radar stations - the Battle of Britain had begun.

RAF Fighter Command responded immediately, sending squadrons of Spitfires, Hurricanes and Blenheims to engage the attacks both at day and night, and a fierce war of attrition raged in the skies over Southern England.

Never in history had the fate of a whole nation rested with such a small group of men. Showing almost unbelievable bravery and a tenacious determination, the RAF fought off the Luftwaffe and thwarted Hitler's plans for invasion. Fewer than 3000 men flew in the Battle of Britain, but by the time it ended, just sixteen weeks later, over 500 RAF aircrew had lost their lives with many more seriously wounded.

"Never in the field of human conflict was
so much owed by so many to so few".

(Winston Churchill. August 1940)

PORTRAITS

B.G. Stapleton

Flying Officer Stapleton came to the UK from South Africa and joined the Royal Air Force in 1939. After initial flying training he was posted to 603 Squadron flying Spitfires.

During his impressive career he shot down ten enemy aircraft, shared in the destruction of a further two and was awarded the Distinguished Flying Cross in November 1940.

During a fierce air battle north of the Thames, his Spitfire was hit in the wing by cannon fire which severed a control cable. Only just able to manoeuvre the plane, he glided down from 18,000ft and crash landed into a field. He emerged from his wrecked aircraft unhurt, and was met by a family of four who had been picnicking in the field - they immediately offered him a cup of tea!

His luck ran out following an attack on a German train that blew up right in front of him damaging his Spitfire engine with shrapnel. The engine seized and he attempted a long glide back over enemy lines, but he crash landed just two miles short of the English positions, and was captured by the German Army. He spent the rest of the war imprisoned in Stalag Luft 1.

On leaving the RAF in 1946 he spent a short time as a Civilian Pilot flying with BOAC before returning to South Africa. He then worked as a Tour Guide in Durban ('the best job he ever had').

P.G. Leggett

Born in 1921, Pilot Officer Leggett began flying at the age of 18 when he joined an RAF Flying School in Scotland. He spent short periods with 615 and 245 Squadrons before flying Hurricanes with 46 Squadron at Stapleford.

During one mission in November 1940, he took off to intercept a formation of Italian bombers flying one of their few sorties to the UK from Melsbroek airfield in Belgium. Having been separated from their fighter escort over the North Sea, the Italians were met by two squadrons of Hurricanes. Pilot Officer Leggett shot down a Fiat BR20 over Ashford in Kent.

In the summer of 1941 he moved to 249 Squadron in Malta, from where he was sent

to engage a formation of Junkers JU88s with Messerschmitt BF109 fighter escort. On take-off he discovered he had no oxygen supply or radio communication, and at 12,000ft he was attacked by BF109s resulting in a cannon shell piercing an oil pipe below the cockpit. With oil in his eyes he escaped back to Malta, but fire broke out en route and he was forced to bale out at a dangerously low 500ft. Fortunately his parachute opened instantly and he landed in soft mud. He was admitted to hospital with leg injuries. Graham Leggett was a Squadron Leader when he left the RAF in 1958.

J.G. Sanders

Flight Lieutenant Sanders joined the RAF in 1936 and after initial flying training joined 111 Squadron as a Hurricane Pilot. Just after the outbreak of war he was made Flight Commander of 615 Squadron stationed at Croydon.

He was to shoot down three enemy aircraft during the squadron's short period in France, and on their return to the UK he went on to destroy a further four German planes.

He was awarded the Distinguished Flying Cross and decorated by King George VI at Kenley towards the end of June 1940.

By the end of the war he is thought to have shot down in excess of fifteen enemy aircraft, and left the RAF in 1947 as a Wing Commander. He went on to a career in insurance.

The Identity Card (pictured left) was carried by James Sanders every day during the Battle of Britain.

R.C. Ford

Sergeant Ford began his distinguished career with basic flying training at Gravesend after joining the RAF Volunteer Reserve. In December 1939 he joined 41 Squadron flying Spitfires from Catterick.

On the afternoon of September 7th 1940, following a dog fight over South Essex, he was shot down with extensive damage to his aircraft and was extremely fortunate to walk clear without injury.

Commissioned as an Officer in late 1940, he was posted to a delivery squadron, but soon volunteered as a pilot with the Merchant Ship Fighter Unit (known as

the 'Suicide Squadron'). Here, his role was to protect merchant shipping convoys by flying a fighter that was launched by rockets from the deck of a ship in the middle of the Atlantic Ocean. Once the attack on the ships was over, he was forced to crash land his aircraft into the sea and await rescue by the Navy. He served on three separate ships, providing protection to shipping convoys on Atlantic crossings and at Gibraltar.

Later in the war, Roy Ford qualified and worked as a Test Pilot and retired from the RAF in 1945. He went on to a highly successful career in banking.

L.W. Harvey

Sergeant Harvey flew Spitfires in the Battle of Britain from Hornchurch where he was stationed with 54 Squadron, and later served with 245 Squadron at Aldegrove before being posted overseas.

It was at this time, whilst in North Africa, that Sergeant Harvey was shot down. A cannon shell pierced a fuel tank close to his cockpit which set both his aircraft and his legs on fire. Attempting to bale out, he found he had no sensation in his lower body and managed to only get clear of his burning Spitfire at very low altitude. As his parachute opened, he looked up to check its condition only to find that this too was alight. Seconds later he hit the ground sustaining severe leg injuries.

Now forced to find shelter behind very low scrub, he evaded capture by an Italian tank that passed within 50 metres and began shooting at him. He was finally picked up by some friendly bedouins on camels and then on to a British Army Bren Gun carrier manned by the 10th Hussars who took him to the RAF Receiving Station at Benghazi.

He recovered from his injuries, was commissioned as an Officer in 1944 and was discharged from the RAF in 1946.

J.C. Freeborn

On joining the RAF in 1938, Flying Officer Freeborn was posted to 74 Squadron at Hornchurch. Thought to have flown more sorties than any other pilot during the Battle of Britain, he had a remarkable career, shooting down ten Messerschmitt BF109s, two BF110s, two Junkers JU88s, a Dornier DO17 and a DO215. He was awarded the Distinguished Flying Cross and Bar for his efforts in protecting Allied troops at Dunkirk and for his part in the Battle of Britain.

During one sortie he went into battle against approximately forty German BF109 fighters. After shooting one down, he himself was hit and crash landed at Manston Airfield with bullet wounds across the top of his head. Fortunately his injuries were not too serious and he made a full recovery.

John Freeborn became Flight Commander at 602 Squadron, and then took command of 118 Squadron until 1944. He left the RAF in 1946 with the rank of Wing Commander.

K.B. Hollowell

Sergeant Hollowell joined 25 Squadron in July 1940 as a Blenheim pilot flying night time missions from North Weald Airfield in Essex.

Ironically, one of the major problems he faced during the Battle of Britain was from 'friendly' ack-ack fire at night, as the Blenheim was often mistaken from the ground for being a hostile Junkers JU88.

During one night mission in August 1940, Sgt. Hollowell lost a propeller over London. Close to stalling speed, he made it back to North Weald, but knowing that by lowering his landing gear the aircraft would lose critical speed, stall and crash, he decided to land with the wheels up. He crash landed, with the aircraft finally coming to rest close to the airfield perimeter fence, giving a rude awakening to

a group of Spitfire and Hurricane crews asleep in tents there. At the end of his first tour, instead of taking leave, he volunteered for duty in the Middle East. After a frustrating wait for orders he ended up on the Gold Coast of West Africa to where various aircraft were shipped in boxes and assembled. He became a 'Ferry Pilot', testing and flying these aircraft (at considerable risk) across the desert to Cairo.

He was awarded the AFC in 1944, and left the RAF in 1945 as a Flight Lieutenant.

J.K. Down

Already in the RAF Volunteer Reserve, Sergeant Down was called to full-time service with the RAF at the outbreak of war. He trained as a Spitfire pilot, and initially joined 64 Squadron, but moved to 616 Squadron at Leconfield in 1940 from where he flew during the Battle of Britain.

During this time he shot down one enemy aircraft and damaged a further two; he then qualified and worked as a flying instructor. After gaining his commission, he left the RAF in 1945 as a Flight Lieutenant, and returned to his family business of importing fruit and vegetables.

John Knight Down is pictured at the top of the photograph (left).

A.C. Leigh

Born in 1920, Sergeant Leigh joined the RAF Volunteer Reserve in the summer of 1939. He qualified as a Spitfire pilot and during the Battle of Britain flew with 64 and 72 Squadrons.

In 1941 he gained his commission and was awarded the Distinguished Flying Medal having completed over 165 flying operations, shot down six Messerschmitt BF109s and shared in the destruction of a Dornier DO17. The citation for his award read:

"His judgement and determination, especially in low flying attacks over northern France, have set an excellent example"   (Sept 1941).

Following a four-month spell in Gibraltar, he joined 56 Squadron back in the UK, but his first operational mission with the squadron ended in disaster. Whilst flying over occupied France, attempting to destroy enemy searchlights, he suffered

damage to his aircraft; as he attempted to fly his stricken Spitfire back to England he had to bale out over the English Channel. He was fortunately rescued by an Allied boat.

Arthur Leigh was awarded the Distinguished Flying Cross in 1944 and left the RAF in 1945 to set up his own building company.

T.N. Hayes

Flight Lieutenant Hayes joined the RAF in the summer of 1939 after already serving three years with 600 Squadron flying Blenheims.

In early March 1940 information was received that the Germans had captured the main airfield in Rotterdam. Thomas Hayes flew one of the six Blenheims that took off from Manston to engage enemy aircraft operating from the Rotterdam airfield. They found nothing in the air but the airfield was full of Junkers JU52s which they dived down to attack. Along with his Commanding Officer he destroyed one with cannon fire. On pulling out of the dive they were attacked by twelve Messerschmitt BF110s. His aircraft was badly damaged with fuel leaking into the cockpit. Attempting to escape he dived down low and got onto a compass course for home, but soon discovered he was on a reciprocal course and flying straight into Germany. He turned and found the sky full of Heinkels and Junker JU52s on which he used up the last of his ammunition. One Junker was seen to go down with its port engine on fire.

His was the only aircraft to return to Manston and he was awarded the Distinguished Flying Cross on the 24th of May.

Thomas Hayes retired from the RAF in 1945 as a Wing Commander.

T.F. Neil

Born in 1920, Pilot Officer Neil joined the RAF Volunteer Reserve in 1938 and was called up for full-time service the following year.

Gaining his commission on the completion of his flying training, he joined 249 Squadron as a Hurricane pilot. Within two months he had participated in the shooting down of over ten enemy aircraft (including Messerschmitts, Heinkels, Dorniers and Junkers). He was awarded the Distinguished Flying Cross and Bar.

His luck finally turned when he had a mid-air collision with another Hurricane and lost the rear section of his aircraft. He baled out miraculously unharmed.

Following several months on operations in Malta, Tom Neil became a Liaison Officer to the US Airforce 100th Fighter Group, which eventually led him to be being awarded the US Bronze Star.

He left the RAF in 1964 having achieved the rank of Wing Commander.

J.H. Duart

Pilot Officer Duart began his flying career in 1938 when he received his Pilot's license and joined the Civil Air Guard. At the outbreak of war he volunteered to join the RAF as an Air Gunner and qualified as an Air Gunner Leader in May 1940.

He was posted with 219 Squadron engaged in night fighter operations flying in Blenheims throughout the Battle of Britain.

During one night time sortie over London, he directed his pilot, using the Airborne Interception Radar, onto an enemy aircraft. They approached from behind too quickly and after a short burst of cannon fire, the pilot was forced to close the engines' throttles to avoid collision. This put the Blenheim into a violent spin, and

P/O Duart opened the hatch to bale out, but soon realised that his parachute had been thrown along the fuselage out of reach. Momentarily he considered jumping without it. Fortunately, the pilot regained control and the hatch was closed with all the crew safely inside.

In 1943 he was posted to Canada as a Senior Armament Instructor, and returned to the UK in 1944 to work in the Ministry of Defence.

Howard Duart left the RAF in 1945 as a Flight Lieutenant to continue his career as a Chartered Accountant.

G.H. Bennions

Pilot Officer Bennions joined the RAF as an apprentice and later qualified as a pilot flying Spitfires with 41 Squadron. He gained his commission in the spring of 1940.

During the Battle of Britain he shot down seven Messerschmitt BF109s and one ME110, but not without great personal sacrifice, for he crash landed twice and was finally shot down in October 1940 suffering grievous injuries. His Spitfire was strafed by a BF109 at 25,000ft, with a cannon shell entering through the side of his canopy destroying his left eye and seriously wounding his arm and legs. Somehow he managed to bale out and landed with part of his skull removed and brain exposed.

He was admitted to the Queen Victoria Hospital at East Grinstead where he endured months of plastic surgery under the pioneering Archibald McIndoe, thus becoming a founder member of the Guinea Pig Club. He was awarded the Distinguished Flying Cross on the very day he was shot down.

On making a full recovery he was once again allowed to fly but in a non-combat role. In 1943 he became the Liaison Officer to an American Fighter Unit in North Africa who were beginning to operate with Spitfires.

George Bennions was released from the RAF in 1946 as a Squadron Leader. He went on to become a school teacher and qualified silversmith.

A.V. Johnstone

Born and educated in Scotland, Squadron Leader Johnstone learnt to fly after joining 602 Squadron (Auxiliary Air Force) in 1934. He entered full-time service in 1939 and eventually took command of 602 Squadron in July 1940. Within eighteen days of doing so he had been involved in shooting down nine enemy aircraft (Heinkels, Junkers, Messerschmitts and Dorniers). He was awarded the Distinguished Flying Cross.

In 1941 he was transferred to duties in the Middle East and then onto Malta where he was a Fighter Controller and Deputy Station Commander. On his return to the UK he attended Staff College, and in early 1945 he was a representative of the Royal Air Force in Washington.

After several more Staff appointments and having been honoured with a CB, Sandy Johnstone left from the RAF in 1968 with the rank of Air Vice Marshal.

A.D.M. Boyd

Flying Officer Boyd learned to fly whilst a student at Trinity College. Called for service at the outbreak of war, and after further flying training, he joined 600 Squadron in 1940 flying Beaufighters on night fighting missions. He shot down five enemy aircraft and was awarded the Distinguished Flying Cross in January 1942.

He was involved in what is thought to be the first radar controlled night interception of the war, when he engaged a floatplane. When he fired at it, his guns malfunctioned, but the plane went down and landed in the Thames Estuary.

Later that year he was transferred to the Headquarters of Fighter Command involved in night fighter training. After one year there he was put in command of 219 Squadron later to be stationed in North Africa. He was to shoot down a

further five enemy aircraft whilst flying from Algiers. He was awarded the Distinguished Service Order in March 1944.

Towards the end of the war Archibald Boyd became Air Attaché to Dublin, but left the RAF in 1946 as a Squadron Leader for employment with the defence company Vickers Armstrong and worked on their first nuclear powered submarine. From there he spent the next twenty years with an engineering conglomerate and retired as Chairman/Chief Executive.

A.H. Piper

Sergeant Piper trained as an Air Gunner, joining 236 Squadron at the beginning of 1940 flying in Blenheims.

During one mission he took off with his squadron from Thorney Island to attack the airfield at Querqueville. His formation met fierce opposition over occupied France, and his Blenheim suffered extensive damage to its tail. His was the only aircraft to return home.

He later joined 218 Squadron flying in Stirlings based at Downham Market in East Anglia. He was rear gunner on a mine laying mission when his aircraft came under fighter attack. During the engagement his machine guns 'over-breached' making them inoperable. Over the intercom he directed his pilot in evasive manoeuvres to avoid attack from behind. After eight frustrated attempts to shoot them down the German pilot broke off. Arthur Piper was awarded the Distinguished Flying Cross.

After the war he trained as a pilot and became a flying instructor. He retired from the RAF in 1958 as a Squadron Leader and became involved in Vintage Club Motor Racing with Jaguars and Alfa Romeos.

J.M. Bentley Beard

Born in 1919, Sergeant Bentley Beard began his career with the RAF Volunteer Reserve whilst working in a bank.

He became a Hurricane pilot at the outbreak of war with 249 Squadron, and he shot down a total of seven German aircraft during the war, but was himself shot down twice. On the second occasion he was seriously wounded which virtually ended his operational career.

John Bentley Beard was awarded the Distinguished Flying Medal and the AFC before leaving the RAF as an Officer in 1946.

S.C. Widdows

Born in 1909, Squadron Leader Widdows joined the RAF aged seventeen as an aircraft apprentice, and trained as a pilot in the early 1930s. He qualified as a Test Pilot and carried out the test flights on the first ever Spitfires and Hurricanes to enter service with the RAF.

During the Battle of Britain he was in command of 29 Squadron, a night fighter unit stationed at Digby in Lincolnshire flying Beaufighters. Whilst there, he shot down a Junkers JU88 that was on a night bombing mission and was awarded the Distinguished Flying Cross.

On one occasion he was scrambled to intercept a German bomber formation, but his aircraft suffered engine failure and began to rapidly lose height. He ordered his crew to bale out, and at only 1,000ft above the ground he climbed out of his cockpit, but caught sight of his Radar Operator struggling with his escape hatch.

Now desperately short of time, instead of jumping out to save himself and leaving his crew member to his fate, he climbed back into the cockpit and prepared for an extremely dangerous crash landing at night. Only just missing a high tension power cable, the Beaufighter landed wheels-up in a field.

Charles Widdows had a very successful career in the RAF, retiring in 1958 with the rank of Air Commodore, and was made a CB the following year. He then worked for ten years in the construction industry before entering politics in Guernsey as a Deputy of St Peter Port.

D. Fopp

Australian pilot Desmond Fopp joined the RAF at the outbreak of hostilities in 1939, joining 17 Squadron at Debden flying Hurricanes.

He shared in the destruction of a German Heinkel aircraft in July 1940, but in September, after shooting down a Dornier, his Hurricane was hit and burst into flames. He baled out with severe injuries and spent three months recovering in hospital. He did not return to flying duties for almost a year, but was eventually posted back to his old squadron in the summer of 1941, shortly followed by a posting to 132 Squadron flying Spitfires.

In 1943 he became Liaison Officer to the United States Air Force advising them in fighter tactics. He was awarded the AFC and became a Flight Instructor on Harvards, an advanced training aircraft used by many Commonwealth countries.

After leaving the RAF five years after the war, he continued his instructing role as a civilian with the Navy, training pilots on the Mosquito fighter bomber.

C.N. Foxley-Norris

Flying Officer Foxley-Norris was born into a military family in 1917. The son of a Major in the Cheshire Regiment, he was a scholar at Winchester and Trinity College where he learnt to fly, and joined the RAF in the summer of 1939. He trained as a Hurricane pilot, joining 3 Squadron for the Battle of Britain, towards the end of which he moved to 615 Squadron at Northolt.

In early 1941, during a defensive patrol mission over Kent, he was shot down by a Messerschmitt BF109. His Hurricane caught fire but he managed to bale out unhurt and returned to his squadron.

Three months later he qualified as a flying instructor, and moved to Canada training new pilots. From there he became a ferry pilot, transporting aircraft across the Atlantic Ocean. He spent the final years of the war on operations flying the Mosquito fighter bomber and was awarded the Distinguished Flying Cross.

After the war, Christopher Foxley-Norris continued his impressive career, holding many distinguished posts within the RAF. He retired in 1974 as an Air Chief Marshal, having been awarded a GCB, KCB, CB and OBE.

P.R. Hairs

Pilot Officer Hairs joined the RAF Volunteer Reserve in 1937, and was given his full-time commission with the RAF at the outbreak of war.

Flying Hurricanes with 501 Squadron from Tangmere, he shot down a Messerschmitt BF109 and shared in the downing of a Dornier DO17. He then qualified as a flying instructor and spent two years in Canada training new pilots.

After periods back in the UK and in India, Peter Hairs left the RAF in 1945 and was awarded an MBE.

W.D. David

Flying Officer David was an outstanding Hurricane pilot with 87 Squadron, for during one month he shot down eleven German aircraft and within the space of five days was awarded the Distinguished Flying Cross (and Bar). He took part in one of the most famous incidents of the Battle of Britain when his wing man was shot down during a dog fight - his friend baled out, but whilst parachuting to safety was attacked by a German BF109 fighter. F/O David spun his Hurricane around and shot the aircraft down, but with this another came in to

attack the stricken pilot, but was fought off. Dennis David's most vivid memory from the Battle of Britain was seeing his friend parachute into the sea, discard his flying kit and swim ashore in a pair of bright blue underpants.

Dennis David went on to have a distinguished military career, and amongst many other achievements he was awarded the AFC in 1943. He was Air Attaché to Budapest during the Hungarian uprising in 1956 and was made a CBE in 1960. He retired from the RAF seven years later with the rank of Group Captain.

A.G. Russell

Sergeant Russell joined the Royal Navy Volunteer Reserve in 1938 but was soon removed from service as he was discovered to be underage. In January 1939 he legitimately joined up, but this time with the Royal Air Force.

In 1940, qualifying as a Hurricane pilot, he joined 43 Squadron at Ulsworth with two friends from his Operational Training Unit. Within three weeks he was the only one left alive.

Along with 120 other pilots he was posted to Malta for a three month tour in 1942. Early one morning he took up three new pilots to allow them to gain operational experience. They were the only ones flying when Control radioed that sixty enemy aircraft were flying straight for them. He led these new pilots towards the sun from where they dived straight through the enemy formation of thirty bombers escorted by a further thirty Messerschmitt fighters. The Hurricanes are believed to have shot down four before returning to base without loss.

Sergeant Russell's tour was extended to nine months by the end of which only thirty of the original one hundred and twenty pilots had survived.

Anthony Russell left the RAF in 1946 as a Flight Lieutenant. He then chose to pursue a potentially lucrative career in banking for, as he says :

"Never was so much owed, by so many, to so few"!

E.W. Wright

Sergeant Wright had an eventful time during the Battle of Britain. He joined 605 Squadron in July 1940, and had achieved a probable score of six enemy aircraft shot down within the first four months with the squadron. He was awarded the Distinguished Flying Medal.

During one of these air battles, he engaged a large formation of enemy bombers. Following his attack he broke away to find the sky suddenly empty of aircraft apart from a small black dot on the horizon. He chased after what turned out to be a stray Messerschmitt BF109. He could not catch up with it, so he fired some speculative shots at it from extreme range. The unlucky German pilot was hit, opened his canopy and baled out. Sergeant Wright circled him in his parachute until he landed in a field and was arrested by farm workers with pitch forks.

He was commissioned as an Officer in December 1940. The following December he was posted to the Far East and suffered the horrors of Japanese imprisonment after being captured in the spring of 1942.

He remained in captivity until the end of the war, and on his return home was awarded the Distinguished Flying Cross.

Eric Wright was given a CBE in 1964, nine years before his retirement from the RAF having made the rank of Air Commodore.

H.P. Patten

Born in 1917, Flying Officer Patten joined the RAF in 1937 and trained as a Spitfire pilot.

One of his most important combat roles was in defence of allied troops at Dunkirk where he shot down a Messerschmitt BF110, and he shot down a second whilst defending RAF Kenley airfield back in the UK.

From Kenley he moved to 307 Squadron, a Polish night fighter unit based at Middle Wallop, from where he shot down a Heinkel HE111.

In 1943 he was posted to RAF HQ Malta where he controlled night fighter operations, and a year later became Flight Commander at 255 Squadron at Foggia where he shot down another enemy aircraft, this time a Junkers JU88.

Hubert Patten left the RAF in 1945 to work for the International Aviation Authority in Paris until rejoining the RAF in 1949 as a Flight Controller. He finally left fifteen years later to work as a civilian with NATO.

T.M. Kane

Flying Officer Kane joined the RAF in 1938 aged 18, trained as a Spitfire pilot and joined 234 Squadron for the Battle of Britain.

In September 1940 he shared in the shooting down of a Junkers JU88, and the following day he shot a Messerschmitt BF109 over the English Channel, but in the aerial fight that followed a cannon shell hit his engine which promptly stopped. He pulled back the canopy, turned his Spitfire upside down and attempted to bale out. Half way out of the stricken aircraft he realised the radio and oxygen supply leads were still connected to him, so he climbed back in, disconnected them and finally got free of the plane at a height of 6,000ft. He now struggled to find his parachute rip-cord, finally pulling it at a perilously low 500ft. (He is estimated to have had only three seconds left to pull the cord before hitting the sea).

He was rescued by a German patrol boat and spent the remainder of the war as a prisoner.

Terence Kane stayed in the RAF after his release but eventually left and became a Senior Civil Servant and later ran a flying club.

P.M. Brothers

Born in 1917, Flight Lieutenant Brothers learnt to fly when still a young teenager, and joined the RAF aged 18. He was posted with 32 Squadron flying Hurricanes and became their Flight Commander in 1938 aged just 21.

There he stayed until 1940, a period during which he destroyed a total of eight enemy aircraft. After joining 257 Squadron at Debden he increased his score by shooting down a further two Dorniers and was awarded the Distinguished Flying Cross in September 1940.

During an attack on an enemy formation, he was forced to manoeuvre his Hurricane so violently that he snapped an aileron control cable, making his aircraft virtually impossible to fly. He limped back to Biggin Hill and prepared for a crash landing. With the cockpit open ready for a quick exit, his 'lucky scarf' was

taken from his neck by the wind. Despite this bad omen he managed to land, and once on the ground, he was relieved to find the scarf safely entwined around a rear section of his aircraft. He can be seen wearing it in the photograph (left). Pete Brothers was to go on to hold many important positions within Fighter Command and was awarded a Bar to his DFC along with a Distinguished Service Order.

After the war he joined the Colonial Service in Kenya but rejoined the RAF in 1949 to continue his impressive career. He was made a CBE and retired from the RAF in 1973 as an Air Commodore.

W.J. Green

Sergeant Green left school aged 15 to work in a cardboard box factory, but by the winter of 1936 he had joined 501 Squadron as an Aero Engines Fitter. Transferring to pilot training at the outbreak of war, he flew Hurricanes throughout the Battle of Britain with 501 Squadron at Middle Wallop.

In August 1940 he attacked a formation of Junkers JU88s over Manston, but was hit by 'friendly' anti-aircraft fire which shot away half of his undercarriage and engine. With oil covering the windshield he managed to crash land at Hawkinge digging the nose of his aircraft into the ground and finishing up in a vertical position. He climbed out totally unharmed.

Nine days later he was shot down while intercepting nearly two hundred BF109s over Deal in Kent. His engine and canopy were hit by cannon fire and he was covered in highly flammable glycol coolant. He baled out at 16,000ft. Falling at over 120mph his boots flew off and he began to uncontrollably tumble through the sky. Pulling the rip cord he rolled into the opening parachute becoming

wrapped up in it. He desperately struggled to free himself and at only 300ft from the ground the wind caught under a fold of silk and billowed the parachute open. He landed in a cow field near Canterbury with leg injuries.

Bill Green returned to flying throughout the war, leaving the RAF in 1947 and the RAF Volunteer Reserve in 1953 for a remarkable career in industry becoming Chairman and Chief Executive of the Crown Group.

A.D. Murray

Squadron Leader Murray joined the RAF before the war, and was posted to 18 Squadron in the spring of 1935 as a pilot on Hawker Hart Bombers. Later that year he transferred to maritime duties, training for catapult launches and deck landings. He then joined 1812 (Torpedo Bomber) Squadron detached to HMS Glorious flying Swordfish floatplanes.

In spring 1940 he converted to flying Hurricanes, spending short periods with 46 and 501 Squadrons before taking command of 73 Squadron at Debden Airfield.

In the winter of 1940 he went to the Middle East, and it was during this time in the Western Desert that Sq/Ldr. Murray took part in the destruction of 16 enemy aircraft on the ground as well as shooting down a Junkers JU88 and a Fiat G50. He was awarded the Distinguished Flying Cross.

He became 'Controller' at Heliopolis (Cairo), taking on the task of locating potential airfields in the desert. On his return to the UK he became Station Commander of RAF Hurn, then on to RAF Tangmere and finally he took command of RAF Manston in the summer of 1944.

Following his distinguished service, Alan Murray retired from the RAF in 1958 as a Wing Commander and began a new career in insurance.

J.D. Bisdee

Educated at Marlborough College and Cambridge, Pilot Officer Bisdee was already a serving member of the RAF Volunteer Reserve before he joined 609 Squadron at the outbreak of war as a Spitfire pilot.

In the summer of 1940 he destroyed a total of four Messerschmitt BF110s and later, during fighter sweeps over northern France, he claimed a further five Messerschmitt BF109s and was awarded the Distinguished Flying Cross.

On taking command of 601 Squadron in 1942 he moved to operations in Malta flying from the American aircraft carrier USS Wasp. During an offensive sortie he was shot down by BF109s, he baled out but on pulling his rip-cord the harness broke leaving him upside down, suspended from his parachute by one leg. After an uneremonious landing in the sea, he spent several hours in his emergency dinghy paddling back to shore.

He was awarded an OBE in 1945, and left the RAF that year with the rank of Group Captain.

R.W. Foster.

Pilot Officer Foster joined the RAF Volunteer Reserve at the start of the war and trained as a Hurricane pilot with 605 Squadron.

During the Battle of Britain he shot down two Messerschmitt BF109s before being posted overseas to Darwin, Australia. Here, he assisted in the fight against the Japanese and shot down a total of six Mitsubishi aircraft and was awarded the Distinguished Flying Cross.

Bob Foster left the RAF two years after the war with the rank of Wing Commander.

D.L. Armitage

Flying Officer Armitage joined the RAF Volunteer Reserve in 1939 flying Spitfires with 266 Squadron throughout the Battle of Britain. Flying from Wittering Airfield he shot down a Junkers JU88, and was awarded the Distinguished Flying Cross.

He was then promoted, and led 129 Squadron still operating with Spitfires.

Dennis Armitage left the RAF at the end of the war with the rank of Squadron Leader. He returned to his former career as an electrical engineer in the Staffordshire coal mines.

W.J. Corbin

Sergeant Corbin joined the RAF Volunteer Reserve in early 1939, and entered full time duty in September of that year as a Spitfire pilot.

He served with 66 Squadron at Coltishall Airfield in East Anglia from where he flew until the end of 1941. He then moved on to an Operational Training Unit as a Gunnery Flight Instructor and gained his commission before joining 72 Squadron in Algiers. Here he shot down a Messerschmitt BF109 and damaged another. He was awarded the Distinguished Flying Cross.

On his return to the UK he became a Chief Armaments Instructor but left the RAF in 1945 as a Flight Lieutenant. He rejoined the Volunteer Reserve three years after the end of hostilities.

P. F. Morfill

Flight Sergeant Morfill joined the RAF in the summer of 1930 as an apprentice, qualified as a rigger, but transferred to flying in 1936. On completion of his flying training he joined 65 Squadron with which he flew for three years, and was posted to 501 Squadron at Tangmere before the Battle of Britain began. He fought in the skies over France destroying two enemy aircraft before the squadron was pulled back to Croydon in June 1940. During that summer he shot down four enemy aircraft, damaged one and shared in the destruction of a fifth. He was awarded the Distinguished Flying Medal.

Later, following an attack on a Dornier 17 off the Isle of Sheppey, he shot down the German plane which crashed into the sea. The aircrew escaped and scram-

bled into their emergency rubber dinghy. Flt/Sgt. Morfill flew over them at very low altitude filming with his gun camera to record the downing. The German airmen leapt out of the dinghy fearing they were under attack from a maverick pilot. They were not, and they all got safely back in the dinghy.

In 1941 he trained as a pilot instructor, spending the last part of the war in Rhodesia. On his return to England he worked for the Ministry of Aircraft Production researching new advances in bomber technology. He left the RAF in 1958 retaining the rank of Squadron Leader.

C.J. Riddle

Flight Lieutenant Riddle flew with 601 Squadron from 1936 with the Auxiliary Air Force before being commissioned into full time service towards the end of 1939.

His initial encounter with the Luftwaffe proved to be a sobering one. During his first combat engagement he attacked a Heinkel bomber over Brussels, and was pleased to see his shooting was very accurate with his cannon fire converging right onto the target. He realised just in time that he was actually looking at the tracer bullets from the Heinkel's gun turret, and it was they who were shooting particularly straight - but straight at him!

Throughout the Battle of Britain he fought alongside his brother, Hugh Riddle, who was also a pilot with 601 Squadron. This led to some confusion at the Air Ministry who on two occasions notified the wrong brother's wife when one had been shot down.

In May 1940 during the air battle over Dunkirk, he scored a 'probable' shooting down of a Messerschmitt BF110, and in September shared in the downing of a Dornier 17.

Christopher Riddle left the RAF in 1946 with the acting rank of Wing Commander. He began work with an international trading company buying timber from Scandinavia. Spending much time in Swedish and Norwegian hotels, he was impressed with the bedding used in these countries, and became responsible for the introduction of the duvet to the UK.

R.M. Hall

Pilot Officer Hall, born in 1917, was accepted for Army Officer training at Sandhurst in 1936, after which he joined the Royal Tank Regiment as a 2nd Lieutenant. In 1940 he transferred to the RAF and after initial flying training he flew with 152 Squadron as a Spitfire pilot.

It was from there that on October 7th 1940, following a dog fight over Lyme Regis, that he ran out of fuel forcing him to crash land in a field. He escaped without injury.

In the winter of 1940 he joined the newly formed 255 Squadron flying Defiants. He claimed the squadron's first ever success when he shot down a Heinkel 111 over the Humber.

He later became Flight Commander of 72 Squadron at Gravesend and in 1942 was posted with 92 Squadron. He was awarded the Distinguished Flying Cross in November 1942, but lost his flying status later that year due to a recurring medical problem and spent the rest of his time in an Administrative Unit.

Roger Hall left the RAF in 1944 as a Flight Lieutenant but rejoined the RAF Volunteer Reserve in 1960.

A.L. Winskill

Pilot Officer Winskill joined 603 Squadron in October 1940 as a Spitfire pilot, and within five weeks had shot down a Messerschmitt BF109, a Heinkel 111 and two Italian Fiat CR42s.

Perhaps one of his most notable achievements during the war was that, despite being shot down twice over enemy occupied territory, he managed to evade capture on both occasions.

In 1941 for example, he was shot down over Northern France during a fighter sweep from Tangmere. Speaking fluent French he quickly located the underground movement who helped him through France and into Spain, from where he was ejected as an 'undesirable alien', and finally home via Gibraltar. He was awarded the Distinguished Flying Cross.

In 1943, having taken the squadron to North Africa, he was forced to ditch his Spitfire in the sea having been hit by enemy flak during a ground attack mission.

He swam ashore and again evaded capture with the help of some friendly Tunisians and returned to his squadron. In 1943 he was awarded the Bar to his DFC.

Archie Winskill was posted back to the UK where he attended Staff College and went on to the Air Ministry.

In 1960 he was given a CBE and retired from the RAF in 1968 as an Air Commodore. He was made a KCVO and worked as Equerry to the Queen and was Captain of the Queen's Flight.

P.H. Fox

In the summer of 1939 Sergeant Fox joined the RAF Volunteer Reserve in Oxford, moving to 56 Squadron the following summer as a Hurricane pilot. At the end of September 1940, during a fierce aerial combat, he was shot down over the Portland area of Southwest England. With his aircraft on fire he baled out with leg injuries but soon returned to his squadron at Boscombe Down.

The following Autumn while flying in the squadron's Magister (a dual control aircraft with no working intercom) there was some confusion between Sergeant Fox and his co-pilot as to who had control of the aircraft. It flew itself into a haystack. Both sustained severe injuries and were admitted to Tidworth Army Hospital.

His run of bad luck continued after joining 234 Squadron when in October 1941, whilst waiting to go home on leave in Oxford, his Commanding Officer asked for

volunteers for low-level attack sweeps on the Cherbourg peninsula in Northern France. An ammunition dump was selected as his target but on crossing the coastline ground fire gained a direct hit on his Spitfire forcing him to crash land. He had considerable trouble leaving the aircraft after the crash as his 'Mae West' life jacket had inflated on impact, pinning him to his seat. He was captured by the German Army, and following two frustrated escape attempts was imprisoned in a cell next to Douglas Bader. Peter Fox was freed in April 1945 by the Desert Rats and returned home to work as a Civil Engineer.

AIRCRAFT REFERENCE

HAWKER HURRICANE

Perhaps the most versatile and robust fighter of the Royal Air Force in 1940, the Hurricane performed superbly well during the Battle of Britain. It accounted for more enemy aircraft shot down than any other.

Specifications

Crew : 1
Speed : 325 mph
Enemy Aircraft shot down : over 1,500

SUPERMARINE SPITFIRE

Descended from racing floatplanes of the 1931 Schneider
Trophy, the Spitfire is often thought to be one of the most
beautiful aircraft in the world. During the Battle of Britain
it also proved to be one of the most deadly.

Specifications

Crew : 1
Speed : 360 mph
Enemy Aircraft shot down : over 1,000

BRISTOL BLENHEIM

Despite being dangerously slow, the Blenheim fought valiantly during the Battle of Britain. It was mainly tasked with night fighter duties and with Coastal Command.

Specifications

Crew : 3
Speed : 290 mph
Enemy Aircraft shot down : 30

LUFTWAFFE AIRCRAFT

Messerschmitt BF109

Dornier DO17

Heinkel HE111

Junkers JU87

Junkers JU88

Messerschmitt BF110

"The gratitude of every home in our Island, in our Empire, and indeed throughout the world, except in the abodes of the guilty, goes out to the British airmen, who, undaunted by odds, unwearied in their constant challenge and mortal danger, are turning the tide of world war by their prowess and devotion. Never in the field of human conflict was so much owed by so many to so few."

Winston Churchill, 20 August 1940

This project could never have happened without the help and support of many people. A few of them are listed below.

Many thanks to -

All my family - *always there.*

The Aircrew and families for their time, humour and hospitality.
Dr David Britain.
Jason Beckwith.
Mary Mullin.
Sheila Bounford.
Clive Barber.
HRH Prince Michael of Kent GCVO.
Kate James.
Jane Moore, Linda Elander and all at The Sunday Times Magazine.
All at Condé Nast.
Malcolm Smith - Battle of Britain Fighter Association.
Terence Pepper - The National Portrait Gallery.
Juliette Fraser and all at NBN International.
David Belson and Bill Hunt - Ministry of Defence.
Kentmere (Photographic Paper Manufacturers) - for their generous support.
Steve Hollamby, Mike Dutch and all at Chandlers Printers.
Mike & Helen.
Chris Dobson.
Sabrina Poma.
Kingsley Jolowicz.
Beth and Karl.
Ben, Jo, John C, Sarah and all at WFCA Integrated.
All at Adams Photographic - Tunbridge Wells.
Scott Bartlett @ Dappa Design.
Sophia Crawford & The Family of Cuthbert Orde.
Ted McMannis - Battle of Britain Historical Society.
Andrew Cormack - The Royal Air Force Museum.

and many, many more.........

Framed Prints

Available direct from the photographer.
For information please Email :

james@jameseckersley.co.uk

or write to :

James Eckersley,
c/o Douglas House, PO Box 396,
Tonbridge. TN9 9BB. UK